Discovering Dinosaurs

Tyrannosaurus Rex

Aaron Carr

LET'S READ
AV²
BY WEIGL™
ADDED VALUE • AUDIO VISUAL

Go to www.av2books.com, and enter this book's unique code.

BOOK CODE

N 815837

AV² by Weigl brings you media enhanced books that support active learning.

AV² provides enriched content that supplements and complements this book. Weigl's AV² books strive to create inspired learning and engage young minds in a total learning experience.

Your AV² Media Enhanced books come alive with...

Audio
Listen to sections of the book read aloud.

Key Words
Study vocabulary, and complete a matching word activity.

Video
Watch informative video clips.

Quizzes
Test your knowledge.

Embedded Weblinks
Gain additional information for research.

Slide Show
View images and captions, and prepare a presentation.

Try This!
Complete activities and hands-on experiments.

... and much, much more!

Published by AV² by Weigl
350 5th Avenue, 59th Floor
New York, NY 10118

Website: www.av2books.com   www.weigl.com

Library of Congress Control Number: 2013937450
ISBN 978-1-62127-242-7 (hardcover)
ISBN 978-1-62127-248-9 (softcover)

Printed in the United States of America in North Mankato, Minnesota
3 4 5 6 7 8 9 0 18 17 16 15 14

012014
WEP030114

Project Coordinator: Aaron Carr
Art Director: Terry Paulhus

All illustrations by Jon Hughes, pixel-shack.com; Alamy: 19 inset, 20.

Tyrannosaurus Rex

In this book,
you will learn

what its name means

what it looked like

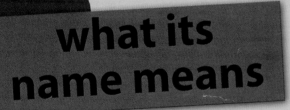

where it lived

what it ate

and much more!

Meet the Tyrannosaurus rex.
Its name means
"tyrant lizard king."

5

Tyrannosaurus rex was one of the largest dinosaurs that ever lived. It was bigger than a school bus.

Tyrannosaurus rex
had a huge mouth.
Its jaw was four feet long.
It had 60 very sharp teeth.

Tyrannosaurus rex
was a meat eater. It could eat
up to 500 pounds of meat
in one bite.

Tyrannosaurus rex
had very small arms.
Its arms were too small
to help it eat.

Tyrannosaurus rex used its strong legs to move quickly.

It may have been able
to run more than
25 miles an hour.

Tyrannosaurus rex
lived in forests near rivers
and swamps.

16

It could be found
across North America.

Tyrannosaurus rex died out more than 65 million years ago.

People know about Tyrannosaurus rex because of fossils.

People can go to museums to see fossils and learn more about the Tyrannosaurus rex.

Tyrannosaurus Rex Facts

These pages provide detailed information that expands on the interesting facts found in the book. They are intended to be used by adults as a learning support to help young readers round out their knowledge of each amazing dinosaur or pterosaur featured in the *Discovering Dinosaurs* series.

Pages 4–5

Tyrannosaurus rex means "tyrant lizard king." It is sometimes called T. rex. As the largest member of the tyrannosaur family of dinosaurs, T. rex was one of the fiercest predators of the prehistoric world. The T. rex is best known for its large jaw, sharp teeth, and powerful hind legs. T. rex was once thought to be the largest of all predatory dinosaurs, but larger dinosaurs, such as Spinosaurus and Giganotosaurus, have since been discovered.

Pages 6–7

T. rex was one of the largest dinosaurs that ever lived. T. rex would have been up to 21 feet (6.5 meters) tall if it had stood upright. Instead, T. rex held its body in a horizontal position, with its head forward and its tail behind for balance. T. rex could be up to 46 feet (14 m) long. It was a heavily muscled dinosaur, weighing as much as 15,000 pounds (7,000 kilograms).

Pages 8–9

T. rex had a jaw that was 4 feet (1.2 m) long and had 60 sharp teeth. The T. rex had teeth that were up to 6 inches (15 centimeters) long, or about the same size as a banana. These teeth were extremely sharp and serrated to help tear through the T. rex's food. With its huge, powerful jaw and long, sharp teeth, scientists believe a T. rex would have had a strong enough bite to tear through the roof of a car.

Pages 10–11

T. rex was a carnivore, or meat-eater, that could eat up to 500 pounds (230 kg) of meat in one bite. Most scientists believe T. rex was a predatory carnivore. This means it hunted other animals for food. Fossils have shown that T. rex ate bones along with meat. Crushed Triceratops bones have been found in T. rex dung.

T. rex had arms that were too small to help it eat. The T. rex had two sharp claws on each of its two short forearms. Despite their small size, the T. rex's forearms were strong enough to hold weights up to 400 pounds (180 kg). However, the arms were likely too short to help T. rex capture or eat prey. This leads some scientists to believe that T. rex may have been a scavenger.

T. rex may have been able to run more than 25 miles (40 km) per hour. No one is sure how fast the T. rex could run, if it could run at all. Some scientists think it could run as fast as 40 miles (70 km) per hour, though most estimates are closer to 25 miles (40 km) per hour. However, other scientists believe T. rex was too heavy to move so fast. They think it could have only managed a fast walk, like an elephant.

T. rex lived in forests near rivers and swamps across North America. T. rex lived in areas that had a great deal of plant life. These swamp forests had many species of trees, grasses, flowers, and other types of vegetation. Such areas attracted large plant-eating dinosaurs, such as the Triceratops and duck-billed dinosaurs. These dinosaurs were the T. rex's preferred food.

T. rex lived more than 65 million years ago during the Late Cretaceous Period. This period ended when a meteor impact wiped out the dinosaurs. All that people know about T. rex comes from fossils. Fossils are formed when an animal dies and is quickly covered in sand, mud, or water. This keeps the hard parts of the body, such as bones, teeth, and claws, from decomposing. The body is pressed between layers of mud and sand. Over millions of years, the layers turn into stone, and the dinosaur's bones and teeth turn into stone as well. This preserves the size and shape of the dinosaur.

People can go to museums to see fossils and learn more about the T. rex. Millions of people visit museums each year to see T. rex fossils in person. Many large museums, such as the American Museum of Natural History, have permanent T. rex displays. "Sue," one of the largest and best-preserved T. rex displays, is found at the Field Museum of Natural History in Chicago.

KEY WORDS

Research has shown that as much as 65 percent of all written material published in English is made up of 300 words. These 300 words cannot be taught using pictures or learned by sounding them out. They must be recognized by sight. This book contains 51 common sight words to help young readers improve their reading fluency and comprehension. This book also teaches young readers several important content words, such as proper nouns. These words are paired with pictures to aid in learning and improve understanding.

Page	Sight Words First Appearance
4	its, means, name, the
6	a, it, lived, of, one, school, than, that, was
9	feet, four, had, long, very
10	could, eat, in, to, up
13	help, small, too, were
14	move, used
15	an, been, have, may, miles, more, run
16	and, near, rivers
17	be, found
18	out, years
19	about, because, know, people
20	can, go, learn, see

Page	Content Words First Appearance
4	lizard, king, Tyrannosaurus rex (pronounced: tye-RAN-uh-SAWR-us rex), tyrant
6	bus, dinosaurs
9	jaw, mouth, teeth
10	bite, meat eater, pounds
13	arms
14	legs
15	hour
16	forests, swamps
17	North America
19	fossils
20	museums

Check out av2books.com for activities, videos, audio clips, and more!

1 Go to av2books.com

2 Enter book code N 8 1 5 8 3 7

3 Explore your Tyrannosaurus book!

www.av2books.com